Buying Power

THE SECRET ART OF NEGOTIATING DEALS IN THE HOSPITALITY INDUSTRY

CHRIS MACKEY

Published by

Business Growth Advisors

SYDNEY, AUSTRALIA

MDA Publishing
Higginbotham Rd
Gladesville, NSW, 2111
Australia

Book Layout © 2021

Buying Power -- 1st ed.
ISBN 978-0-6450942-4-4

Dedicated to everyone who has been told
that you are slow at learning.

Written by a young boy who grew up in Griffith NSW
Australia, left school at 14 years and 7 months because
his Dad said he was really not good at school.

It wasn't until later in life that I discovered that I was
not "slow", I was just not diagnosed as dyslexic.

I find it impossible to read the way others do, and
spelling is even more of a challenge.

We have other skills which more than compensate for
dyslexia.

If you are like me and want to write a book, you will
find the way to communicate your authority.

Let us never negotiate out of fear.
But let us never fear to negotiate.

JOHN F KENNEDY

ABOUT THE AUTHOR

Chris Mackey is a wholesale and retail veteran & ActionCOACH Business Coach with more than forty years' experience in senior management roles for a variety of Australia's leading businesses.

His expertise includes National Marketing and Promotion Manager for a top 50 ASX company; General Manager of Campbell's Cash and Carry; launching the IGA Supermarket brand in Australia; and extensive international business operations training.

He now shares his wealth of knowledge to empower others to succeed in running their businesses. As an ActionCOACH Business Coach, he helps individuals recognize the value of their unique skills and to find creative solutions to their business challenges.

ACKNOWLEDGEMENTS

When writing a book, there are so many people you wish to say "thank you" to.

To Brett Odgers, my writing coach, Cathy McBurney, and to my editors and proofreaders, thank you for your assistance.

TABLE OF CONTENTS

CHAPTER ONE

BUYING POWER

In this book you will learn how the top businesses around the world negotiate with their suppliers, and you will find out what you are missing out on. As a bonus, when you follow this process you will also build stronger business relationships.

This book is based around my 40 years of experience in retailing and wholesaling, first as a buyer myself and then in leading teams and eventually divisions of buyers.

The question I have for you is "Are you paying too much for your inventory or materials?".

It is understandable that you only know what you know. However, you have been a negotiator all your life. From the day you were born, you have been negotiating with your parents, then family and friends. You went to school and negotiated with your teachers, then got a job…… etc. I think you get the picture!

Wouldn't it be fantastic to be able to increase these negotiating skills? Wouldn't you like to be known as the best negotiator?

Is your chef in control of what stock you buy and where you are buying it from? I know how temperamental they can be, and how finicky. You may wish to go in a particular direction, but you know you're going to get significant pushback from your chef.

Five years ago, I was running a training course for a group of account executives in Sydney who all thought that they were pretty hot-shot negotiators. Part of the course was about how to build stronger relationships with their buyers. I took them to the Flemington Fruit Market in Sydney and gave them all $25.00 and told them to go and create as much value as they could.

Negotiating with the vendors in the fruit market - simple, right?

My hunch was that the tomato seller in the market was going to just eat them up and spit them out, which is exactly what happened. You see, he negotiates for a living. It is his whole life. His success depends on the margin he makes. This is one of the things that I'm going to try to impress upon you in this book.

I find that when I am teaching negotiating to business owners in the hospitality industry, they often feel that suppliers will see them as simply cash grabbers and that their reputations are going to be damaged, particularly in regional communities.

If you are paying too much for your inventory, here are three reasons to take action today:

1. The growth of corporate giants in your industry is really starting to annoy you.
2. You have never started to negotiate with your suppliers because you don't know the process to use, or where to start.
3. You would like to take your business to the next level.

Building a robust process to get you some buying power is an integral part of creating more profit in your business. This will become more evident as you go through this book.

This book is not full of academic theory. Most of what I will show and teach you is based on a real-life case study of my client Alice, owner of A1 Hospitality, a business that includes a hotel, café and five-star restaurant, in a regional part of Australia. While working with me and following the process outlined in this book, she was able to reduce the cost of her inventory by 13%.

It is also based on the fact that I was one of the top buyers within the grocery wholesaling industry in Australia.

So, I promise, as long as you don't take shortcuts, everyone wins.

Negotiating is very similar to baking a loaf of bread. If you don't follow the recipe, or don't allow it to rise, you won't get the results you are looking for. The same is true for the teachings and guidance in this book - you can't take a shortcut. You have got to follow the process, and the reason is that the process works. It will work for you, as it has worked for many others that I have taught it to.

THE SYSTEM MODEL.

A FOUNDATION	B PROCESS
1. RESEARCH 2. LANGUAGE 3. LEADERSHIP	1. MAPPING ALL SUPPLIERS 2. KEY BUYER OF INFLUENCE 3. IDENTIFY NEGOTIATION PARTS 4. PREPARE INITIAL AGREEMENT ON NEW NEGOTIATION PARTS 5. NEGOTIATION PHASE (ROUNDS OF MEETINGS) 6. CLOSE THE DEAL 7. OPTIMISATION PHASE.

I encourage you to follow and complete these steps in the sequence that I am going to guide you through.

I have a significant history as a buyer, first working for Coles Supermarkets for many years, then later for Metcash, Australia's largest grocery wholesaler. I worked at Metcash for nearly 25 years, first as a senior buyer, then as Merchandising Manager responsible for teams of buyers. Ultimately, I was responsible for leading divisions of buying teams across the whole of Australia.

During my time with Metcash, I attended numerous negotiating skills courses and have a certificate in negotiating from the Mount Eliza Business School in Victoria, Australia. Negotiation is a great skill to have and it is something that you will never not use. This by itself is worth the price of this book!

However, even more importantly, after finishing this book, you will have the insights and knowledge used by the top buyers in businesses around the world.

CHAPTER TWO

FIGHT BACK

I was once the seafood buyer for Coles Supermarket chain in Australia.

Retailing is super competitive as you can imagine, and every retailer is trying to get a price advantage over the competition.

At strategic times of the year, the lead up to Easter being a good example, we would have our agents buy up as much frozen, cooked prawns as possible to lock in the best prices we could. This amounted to hundreds of tons of prawns, or shrimp, if you are reading this from the Northern Hemisphere.

This is a case of supply and demand being demonstrated. There will be a shortage of prawn supply, and therefore any stock remaining that Coles did not require will be at a high price.

As an Independent Operator it is difficult to compete against the market dynamics of supply and demand. This is happening in every category in your hospitality business. The supply and demand economy also extends to your team as well.

The above example is one way that, simply by their size, corporate big business can influence your profitability and how successful you are.

If an Independent Retailer wishes to remain competitive with prawns/shrimp at Easter, they will have to pay more than Coles Supermarkets did for stock and then reduce their margin to be close to Coles' retail prices.

Corporate business can influence your ability to have a profitable business in many ways, now and in the future. Some are obvious, like buying up venues near yours, and others are more subtle, like not being on a level playing field when it comes to your cost of goods.

Business owners wear a number of hats every day. Administration for example, is very important, but no one has ever retired wealthy by being great at this. Is there anywhere in your business right now that you can earn an extra $100,000 with the only expense being your time, your passion and your skill set?

If $100,000 isn't enough, then consider that sum multiplied by ten. Has a million dollars got your attention? What could you do an extra one million dollars over ten years??

There is a lot you can do with the income that will flow into your business - not just this year, but also in the years to come.

Corporate companies are squeezing you from the top through competition on your top line revenue. It is no secret that Woolworths in Australia has been heavily investing in the hospitality sector and squeezing independent operators, as they do, in independent retailing. They are also squeezing you on the bottom line as well.

Market leading corporate businesses have an effect on your buying price. This effect is not always obvious; however, they will have negotiated with their suppliers for efficiencies in their supply chain.

They are using their buying power to do better deals.

Your suppliers are in a catch-22 situation. Often what discounts they pass on to their corporate business is recouped through their independent operators.

I know this because I was guilty of doing exactly that in my career in buying for Australian Wholesalers and Retailers.

Would you like to learn the negotiation skills that the large corporations have, without damaging the relationships you have with your suppliers?

Your reputation as a businessperson is paramount, especially if you live in a regional town, as I did, or in a CBD of a major city. I will demonstrate how your business relationships can be strengthened through learning how to negotiate.

There are many ways to grow your business, including adding more outlets; giving your customers a better dining experience; better service; and more offerings. However, as your business grows, the way to increase your margin is by also reducing the cost of your inventory. In other words, widen the gap.

The growth of Woolworths in Australia, into the hospitality sector hasn't just crept in overnight.

A lot of your livelihood is going to be dependent on you being able to compete on a level playing field. Wouldn't you sleep better knowing that there was a way to accomplish this?

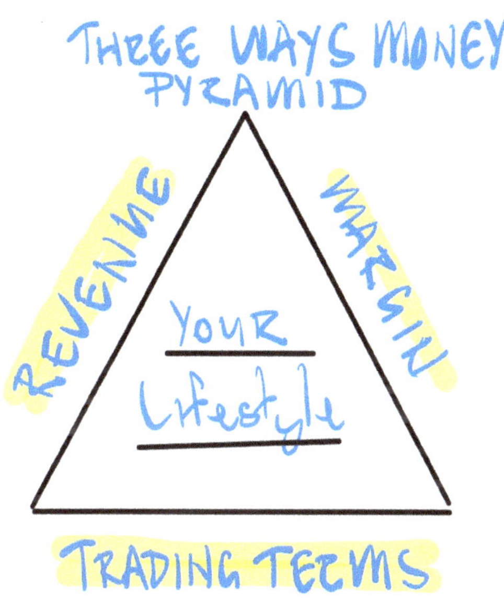

There are three ways that money comes into your business.

The first is through revenue and the second is through the margin, sometimes known as gross profit.

The third and lesser-known way money comes into your business is through your buying power and your ability to negotiate with your vendors and suppliers for favorable trading terms.

Ultimately, the profits from your business fund your lifestyle - the holidays you take; the toys you have; the houses; and the retirement that you are planning for. Having a better understanding of how to use your buying power will help you bring more money into your business, giving you more profit for the lifestyle you want.

I would like to introduce a friend of mine to you. His name is **Macroties** and he is a wise old martini drinking guide that will appear throughout this book at places where I really want you to pay attention to the lesson.

You can imagine old **Macroties** right now speaking to you about this very important topic.

Macroties shares just one profound word.

In the case study from A1 Hospitality Group, that I'm going to refer to throughout this book, I introduce the idea of negotiating with your suppliers for ongoing rebate payments. These payments are a percentage of the money your business spends with them on goods and services, to be paid to you in the form of a fixed percentage. My client Alice, owner of A1 Hospitality Group, did exactly that and, over 12 months, reduced her costs by $130,000 on her purchases of $970,000. I think these are very impressive numbers.

For example, if you purchase $100,000 in goods for the month, you get a 10% rebate. The supplier will pay you $10,000 and, in many cases, you can deduct the $10,000 discount from the total amount you pay.

Let's get back to the case study. At the beginning of our coaching relationship, I suggested to Alice that she needed to negotiate for rebates. This blank shock, horror came over her face. "Rebates", she said, "Rebates!? That's something we don't want to get involved in."

Let me explain why we negotiate for rebates and why rebates are your buying power.

Let's say that you own a restaurant and negotiate with your wholesaler to reduce the price of a box of lettuce by $10.00.

Well, that agreement sounds good until you buy your next box of lettuce. However, lettuce is fresh produce, and a lot of factors influence the cost - seasonal conditions etc. If what you are asking for is dollars off, there is no way that you can know with certainty that you have the best deal. Equally suppliers, over a period of time, will raise their prices to recoup that discount they gave you. Trust me, it happens.

Another reason is that, unfortunately, there are no secrets. If your supplier does give you $10 off a box of lettuce, somehow, someway, one of your competitors will eventually get to see an invoice that shows their lettuce is $50 and your lettuce is $40. Suddenly your supplier has got mud on his face and your competitor leverages them for a better deal as well. The whole thing then falls to pieces.

This is why rebates are the key to buying power. By negotiating for rebates, you receive a discount off your total monthly purchases.

After the blood came back into Alice's face, she started to understand that the best way she could remain in business was to be competitive, and on a level playing field. To do this she needed a healthy margin. There was revenue available to her, she just needed some skills and a process to follow with confidence.

In this book you will learn how to ask for percentage discounts and the way to leverage them for your long-term growth.

CHAPTER THREE

MINDSET

Products don't fail; systems don't fail; procedures don't fail; people do.

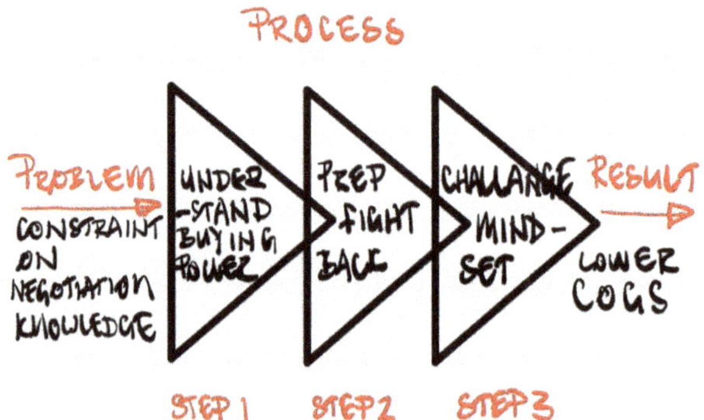

Whatever you are telling yourself about the process of negotiating with your suppliers for rebate payments, you can start changing your mindset today.

How much cash are you leaving on the table, each week, by not engaging with your suppliers?

At this point, your subconscious is going to do its best to sabotage you.

Perhaps you live in a regional or metropolitan community. Your subconscious might be telling you that by just growing your revenue, you will be more profitable; that maybe you can develop a new product, even put in some craft beer and things will be okay.

You don't need to pay attention to these thoughts. They are simply ways that our minds can play tricks on us.

However, now is not the time to walk away. What you are experiencing is fear.

An acronym for fear is:

F- false

E-expectations that

A-appear

R-real

If you have ever wanted proof that you should be learning or improving your negotiating skills, just look around at the family hospitality businesses closed or closing since COVID-19 arrived on our shores.

How many businesses in your industry would have survived if the cost of their inventory was 10% less?

How many of those businesses would have survived if they could have used that money in their cash flow?

Brad Sugars, the founder of ActionCOACH, the world's # 1 business coaching firm, has said "You have to learn before you earn". Are you prepared to work on yourself?

You are going to be challenged here to learn new skills, and to discover how to ask for a better deal.

A great book that I recommend you read is "Getting to Yes. Negotiating an agreement without giving in", written by Roger Fisher, William Ury and Bruce Patton. It is a great introduction to the art of negotiating.

CHAPTER FOUR

THE ART OF EVERYONE WINS

What does win-win actually mean and how do you achieve it in a negotiation?

Many people believe that negotiations end with one party getting little or nothing, while the other party gets most or all of what they want. This is not a win-win outcome.

When negotiating for rebates, the objective is for you to receive what you want and for your supplier to achieve what they want.

It's often easier to understand what a win - win in a negotiation is by demonstrating what it is not.

We can all possibly relate to buying a new car at some point in the past.

Imagine arriving at the car dealership and let's just, for this example, say it is a Land Rover you would like to buy.

You have done your homework on the model you like and the technical features and are close to knowing exactly what it is you are looking to purchase.

The salesperson approaches you and explains the great end of month deal they have for you. You go to their office and the bargaining begins. Does that sound familiar? How does that make you feel?

The salesperson has not asked a lot about your needs, your budget, if you are you ready to buy now or later. On the other hand, you have not asked how their sales month is going, nor whether financing through the dealership will benefit them.

Both of you have taken positions solely based around price, what the salesperson wants as a sales price versus what you want as a purchase price.

The salesperson never once asked how many Land Rovers you have previously owned, in order to calculate your lifetime value to the brand.

Can you see that, in this example, there is no win-win, just simply a sales transaction?

Negotiating so that both parties win is what you are here to do. This is why your suppliers will be happy to enter into a rebate agreement with you.

I can't stress enough how important this is. You need to understand how and what you are prepared to trade off, in order to close the negotiation.

"But what if my supplier doesn't want to negotiate with me or plays dumb and the negotiation stalls?"

Throughout the next chapters of the book, I will show you to how to address this.

Your suppliers need to understand that you have their interests, as well as your own, in mind as you negotiate with them for rebates and, that working closely with your business, will be mutually beneficial.

Let's summarise some of the takeaways so far into three steps:

1. We all need to be open to learning new skills.
2. Understand that it feels really good when you reach a deal and shake hands, knowing that you truly have negotiated something you are proud of.
3. When working in collaboration with your supplier, one plus one doesn't equal two, it can equal five. You have created more value for each other than before you closed this deal.

You have got a new partnership and together you both grow.

One of the first books on negotiating I ever read was "How to Win Friends and Influence People" by Dale Carnegie.

I highly recommend you grab a copy and brush up on your skills. It is a classic management book that has stood the test of time.

By studying Dale Carnegie's book, you will discover new skills on how to overcome objections when negotiating.

Luckily, you have the luxury of not being the first in your market to ask for rebates.

Let's think about that for a second. In particular, Woolworths, the market leading supermarket in Australia, has done you a favour.

If you are negotiating with is a supplier to a corporate organization like Woolworths, I can 100% promise you, they are paying rebates to that organization.

When your supplier tells you that they don't understand what you mean by a rebate, I'm sure they're not lying to you - it is more likely that they just don't understand the terminology.

However, if anyone that you are negotiating with supplies a corporate entity in the food service industry, they have entered into an agreement for some degree of preferential treatment.

I have completed multiple negotiating courses throughout my career and now conduct workshops and courses myself. It is a valuable skill to have and will help you immensely in your business life.

CHAPTER FIVE

GET INTO ACTION

When it comes to getting moving, having the wisdom of Yoda in Star Wars, certainly would be an advantage.

It is time to get organized and take the first steps. Don't let procrastination steal your dreams.

Done is better than perfect.

However, you can't start this process until everything is in order. The key is to remember the five Ps of planning:

1. Proper
2. Planning
3. Prevents
4. Poor
5. Performance

Okay, it's time to start.

1. List all of your vendors on an Excel spreadsheet. If you have another similar software application, that will work just as well. The purpose is to be able to see all your vendors in one location.

2. In a new column, list what goods each vendor supplies you with (for example poultry or general cleaning).

3. Next, in a separate column list your annual purchases at invoice value.

This is the starting point. You might be surprised by how many vendors you actually have!

It is here that you might start to feel a bit overwhelmed by the task at hand. Alice, the business owner in my case study, told me it was at this point she worried that she wasn't ready to commit to the time this process would take her. It took a leap of faith from Alice, and a gentle nudge from me, to get her into action.

Instead of sabotaging yourself by procrastinating at this point, I urge you to push forward. It's okay if not every vendor is on your spreadsheet. What is key here is to take action. Start the process, commit the time, and most of all, enjoy learning some new skills.

BE x DO = RECEIVE is a formula for success.

You have identified what you want to **RECEIVE** (lower COGS in the form of a rebate payment). You will learn the skills to complete the **DO** (the negotiations). However, who do you have to **BE** - someone who commits and sees things through, someone who will rise above obstacles.

Look at the weight loss industry, for example. To lose weight, your **DO**, you have to exercise more and eat less. However, unless you see yourself as one size smaller and act as if you are, your **BE**, then your success will be limited.

BE the person who rises above challenges and finds ways to solve complex issues.

Now that your Excel spread sheet is populated with the data, it is time to review your vendors. What we are looking for is how many duplications there are. For example, how many lettuce suppliers do you have? For every vendor, there are invoices generated; accounts that have been opened; credit applications filled in; not to mention invoice claim disputes for wrong pricing received or goods short delivered. In other words, there is a lot of unnecessary duplication.

These observations should make it worth the time you took to complete the spread sheet!

There is no "magic number" for invoice processing costs - it depends on who is doing the tabulating. The research firm Sterling Commerce put the average cost of processing an individual invoice at between $12 and $30, while other firms place it as high as $40.

You can get a more precise estimate of your own manual invoicing cost by examining:

- Total invoice processing time (including time in the post).
- Total time spent reviewing invoices.
- Total time spent identifying and correcting data entry errors, duplicate payments, etc.
- Storing and shipping costs for physical invoices.
- Discounts lost and penalties incurred due to late payments, errors, etc.
- Total hours of labour spent by staff performing invoicing duties rather than their assigned functions.

Armed with this information, you can then calculate your own estimated average cost of processing invoices by adding together staff costs, discounts lost, late fees paid, storage costs and any postal costs, then dividing that amount by the total number of invoices processed.

If you would like additional information, I recommend you visit:

https://www.purchasecontrol.com/blog/invoice-processing-cost/

Now look over your Excel spreadsheet for duplications. What consolidation could you do to reduce the number of vendors you have? If your hospitality business has a lot of vendors, it is likely for some historical reason – perhaps, for example, the head Chef felt he needed to spread his purchases around town. However, it is time to start making some hard decisions on who gets culled. You would rather be a big fish in a little pond than a little fish in a big pond.

Now it is time to draw up a trading term agreement document that both you and your vendor will sign off on, after you have completed the negotiations together. In a later chapter, I will go into more details.

There is a reason that big business is big business - they cannot manage processes without documentation. As I advised my client Alice, from A1 Hospitality, you can't do deals anymore based on handshakes. Your business is a professional hospitality operation, and as such there must be professional documentation.

However, there are no requirements to involve lawyers (and their associated costs) in a trading term agreement, as it is not a contract. The difference is that either party, as long as they both agree, can make alterations to an agreement. Unlike a supply contract, it is not legally binding and there is also no penalty if the agreement is broken by either party, other than loss of revenue and reputation.

It is a tried and tested method of keeping costs down and still achieving the outcome of having a document whereby each party has a clear understanding of what the details of the agreement are.

As a thank you for purchasing this book, you can download the process map free of charge.

Go to: https://mailchi.mp/9c33b2b1bdf4/buying-power-download

CHAPTER SIX

ROUND ONE OF THE NEGOTIATIONS

In a perfect world, your vendors and suppliers would walk into your office unsolicited and offer you a better deal than what you asked for. Adding to that, they would give you even better deals each year thereafter.

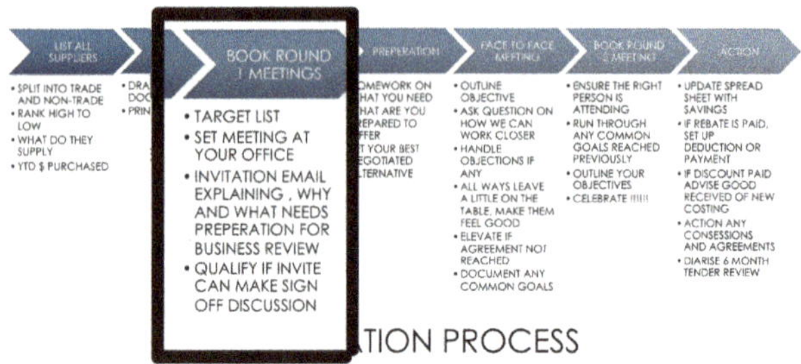

In my buying career this only happened to me once. At the time, the company I was working for was just starting to establish itself in the Australian marketplace. Our current supplier was one of the big two breakfast food manufacturers and they understood that new owners always ask for a better deal. They had the foresight to offer a better deal before they were asked and, from that day forward, we had a better relationship with them than any of our other suppliers. If they asked for a favour, our answer was always YES!

Expect the unexpected. If one or more of your suppliers offers you a rebate payment, establish the best relationship with them that you can. You will be surprised at how quickly all your other suppliers find out. Jealously is a good motivator!

In this chapter we are going to look at how to begin negotiating with your suppliers – what I call Round One. The purpose of this stage of our negotiation process is to state your intention and to set up the next meeting.

When negotiating, we often think that the purpose of the first meeting to get a result or an outcome. However, in this instance, it is simply to get to the next meeting.

The first meeting is about stating your intention to have a negotiation and to engage the support of your suppliers in helping you achieve your goals. Think of it as a first date - you would not likely ask "How much to do you earn?". It's the same for this key step in the negotiation process.

Most of the time your suppliers will tell you a story - how they don't have the authority to give you a better cost; or that you are already getting the best price, etc. This is all part of the negotiating process and I would be surprised if it doesn't happen. However, once you can find out what your supplier wants from you in return for the rebate you are requesting, it is amazing how you both can say YES.

In this first meeting, you are going to be fact finding. You need to ask whether the person you are sitting with has the authority to do this deal. If the answer is NO, then you need to ask for the general manager or, even better, the owner of the business to attend the next meeting. They need to know that you are serious about this.

During this meeting you are building a system or process. The advantage of having a process is that you can go back along the different steps to understand where any problems occurred and what you need to do to correct them. What changes to your language do you need to make?

Something to keep in mind though, is that having a process doesn't mean you have to use all of its steps each time. If you are getting signals that your supplier is willing to negotiate and reach a deal for a rebate right away, then ask for it. For example, "I want a 15%, or 10% rebate paid to us each month. Is this something that you can help me with?" They might just say YES.

Tom Peters is an expert at selling and is the author of many great books. Tom's whole teaching is based around building trust. I suggest you have a read of some of his work.

Trust between you and your supplier is what we are building during this first meeting. People will do a deal with you if they know you, they like you, and they trust you.

Can you clearly tick all those boxes - know, like and trust? Building trust starts with you and your supplier getting to know and like each other on a more personal level.

What are your common likes and interests? Do both of your children play soccer; do you love good wine; do you belong to similar organizations, etc.? Once you can say YES to knowing and liking, then the third part is trust. This is something that might be easily given but once broken, is very hard to get back.

A good way to find out whether a supplier likes you or not is by phoning them. If they answer or you are put through to them right away, this usually means they like you. If you have trouble getting hold of them, then they probably don't like you that much!

As our guide Macroties said at the beginning of this chapter, "Slow and steady gets the yes".

Remember, the purpose of the first meeting is to get to your next meeting. Your next meeting might not be with the person who is sitting in front of you, however, there is a next meeting.

It's critically important that you understand that this is a tactic and is exactly what happens every year in fast moving consumer goods industries, known as FMCG.

How do I know this? It was my job when I worked for Coles Supermarkets as a buyer and then for Metcash Trading as a senior buyer, ultimately leading divisions of buyers across Australia. This is also exactly what Woolworths, Aldi, Costco and Bidvest do with all of their suppliers.

Each year, all national and multi-national retailers and wholesalers sit down with their suppliers and vendors and negotiate for a better deal. This is also what you need to be doing!

CHAPTER SEVEN

FAIL TO PLAN, PLAN TO FAIL

You have new skills in negotiations, and now you have a plan to follow. You have brushed up on a few of the extra materials, and I hope you are reading some of the books on negotiating that I suggested.

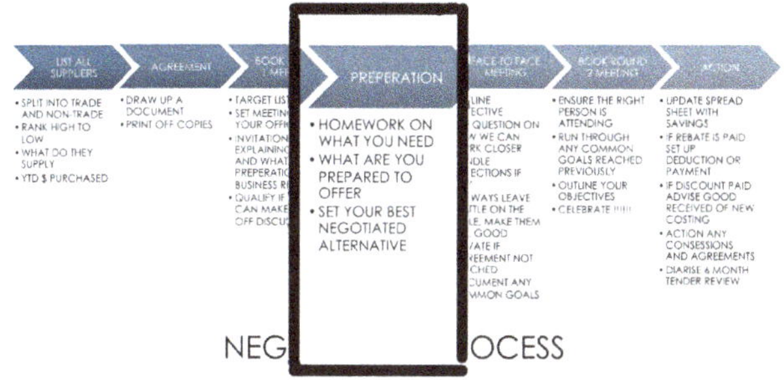

At this point in the process do you have butterflies in your stomach? Are you perhaps feeling a little queasy?

Before we go into round two of the negotiations, let's address the elephant in the room.

Are you worried that the first time you ask for a better deal from your vendor that you will get a **NO** instead of a **YES**?

When you feel these butterflies, understand your subconscious is trying to sabotage you again. At this point, if you are worried about getting a **NO**, you might decide to abandon the whole project.

It is important for you to understand that your concerns are very natural, and it happens to almost everyone at some point when learning a new skill.

The advice I have to offer is to keep focusing on the stage of the process you are at.

It's a lot like playing competitive golf. The golfers who have the lowest handicaps have disciplined their minds to put all their focus on hitting the shot at their feet, even if it is off in the rough.

The golfers that let their minds race with thoughts of winning the club championship; how many strokes to the pin; or how many strokes they have had so far will be far less successful.

To avoid worrying about your vendor saying **NO** to your request for a rebate, let's just focus on this stage of the process. Also, if your motivation is being challenged, remember that reducing your costs will help secure your future and the future of all your team.

In round one of your meetings, you hopefully learned a lot about your supplier by asking open ended questions. Was the idea of forming a formal supply arrangement with you something they would be open to? Did you find out if they were authorised to sign off on such a deal, or was there someone more senior who made those kinds of decisions?

You may also have discovered if their business is looking to grow significantly in the near future and what, if any pain points, they currently have that you could solve for them.

The best "softening" questions are open-ended ones. These are the kind of questions that require a response to be more than just a "yes" or "no". These questions usually contain who, what, when, or how.

Example:
- "How did you find new clients?"
- "What do you think of the latest acquisition by a big corporate?"
- "How long have you been a supplier to a corporate competitor of ours?"
- "With all of the features and advantages I have pointed out, what is the best way forward for both of us?"

This next step in the process is where you start to rehearse your next negotiation, get your thoughts down on paper and out of your head. By doing this you are creating new pathways for learning in your brain. You are developing muscle memory.

You may be thinking that you can skip this part. Perhaps you don't see the need to do any pre-planning before your next meeting.

However, as I said previously, a successful negotiation is much like baking a cake. If you skip one of the steps the cake is not going to rise.

Now is the time to consider all your options.

We have already mentioned the win-win. However, we also need to consider when to walk away from the negotiations. This is equally important because sometimes they don't go the way you want them to and knowing when to walk away is critical.

There is a terminology in negotiations called BATNA:

Best
Alternative
To
A
Negotiated
Agreement

Your BATNA is your no-deal option - the point where you stand up, shake the person's hand, and say "Thank you, it's clear that we can't reach an agreement today.

I'm going to stop these negotiations and we will re-group and meet up again in the future."

If you can't reach an agreement, then there are only 3 options left open to you:

1. Stop all buying from that supplier.
2. Move them to unfavourable payment terms or some other situation that works better for your business that your supplier's.
3. Escalate the negotiation to someone more senior in the organisation.

The only option you must not use is to have your bluff called and you take no action.

Once you have a firm commitment to yourself on what your no deal point is, you need to give some serious consideration to what points and concessions you are willing to make in return for a better deal as a percentage rebate.

Below are some of the action steps you should consider, but not limit yourself to:

Consolidate the number of suppliers you have in one category.

I don't know too many vendors or suppliers who are not looking for additional sales without having to bring on an additional customer. This concession is of greatest importance to your suppliers.

For example, let's say you are purchasing a hundred thousand dollars' worth of fresh produce a year, and you get this produce from three different vendors, paying each of them approximately $33,000.

If you offered to purchase all that fresh produce from the vendor you want deal with, you would triple their business. Then, in return, you ask for a 10% rebate.

Tripling the supplier's business without any additional spending on their part for marketing expenses to find new customers or for labour, is a seriously compelling argument!

Early payment discounts.

Post Covid-19, cash has never been as important to a business as it is now, especially in the very hard-hit hospitality industry. The tourist trade has never, in our living memories, been so challenging. Therefore, cash flow for your vendors and suppliers is absolutely critical to them.

Your advantage is you get paid as soon as a sale is completed - you don't have to issue an invoice and wait 30 days to get paid for it.

Depending on your situation, you may be able to improve your supplier's cash flow significantly, which is a massive win for them.

For example, let's say you are paying your vendor's invoices 30 days from the end of the month, or 14 days from the end of the month, or perhaps you only pay when they call.

Whatever your system is, think about how much of a benefit it would be for your vendor, who might be struggling with cash flow right now, if you said "Okay, our win-win is that I can pay you 14 days from the end of the week".

You can offer a 14-day account instead of a 30- day and have no negative impact on your cash flow position.

I hope this is starting to make sense about the win-win in your negotiations, and how relationships are important. You are in a position to really change your supplier's destiny - you just don't know how important cash flow is to them. This might cement your relationship more than anything else.

Consolidate deliveries into one location if your business has multiple sites.

Perhaps the delivery could go to your main distribution centre instead of three sites. This could save your vendor hours of driving. You can calculate the savings for them.

This may not be practical. However, in the case study from A1 Hospitality, my client Alice had her different businesses in the same precinct, but the vendor had to drive 200 meters to each different location. As a side benefit, consolidating the deliveries led to savings for Alice as well. The receiving dock was opened less, equating to reduction is labour hours; there was only one invoice to process instead of three; there was tighter security on checking for short deliveries on invoices and incorrect charges. As you can see, there are a multitude of negotiating points you can come up with.

Demonstrate the features, advantages and benefits that entering into an agreement will have for your supplier.

These might include facts such as your growth in the market has been outstanding and you expect to grow continuously at the same rate; your business is in the best location; you have consistently paid your invoices on time, etc. These should be documented into a PDF for the supplier to take away and consider. Everyone likes a winner and it's your job in the next round of the negotiation to help your supplier understand that you are going up and they need to be with you for the long term.

As you can see, there is a lot to consider before you have your round two meeting! Now is the time to think about what your vendor possibly wants from you and what you are prepared to offer to close the deal.

Negotiating has been a large part of my life. The relationships I built have stood the test of time and I am very blessed by them.

It has been 10 years since I have left senior management in the grocery industry, but I am still in regular contact with some of the industry leading CEO's. We use LinkedIn to stay in touch and we catch up for beers whenever possible. None of these relationships would exist if I had not known how to build them though negotiating win-win agreements.

Here is a summary of what has been discussed in the planning and preparation stage of negotiations:

- We have acknowledged your potential concerns about hearing a NO from you vendor and have offered strategies to manage your mindset.
- You know a lot more about your supplier's issues and concerns after your first meeting with them and you have written down your notes in summary form.
- You have a clear understanding of what your BATNA: Best Alternative To A Negotiated Agreement is. Knowing when to walk away is more powerful than doing a lose-win deal.

A list of what concessions you are prepared to make in the next round of meetings has been documented.

The top three recommendation I have made are:
1. Consolidate your vendors.
2. Early payment discounts.
3. Consolidate deliveries into one location.

Documenting your business's features, advantages and benefits in a PDF presentation forms a compelling argument as to why your vendor should partner with you for the long term.

CHAPTER EIGHT

ROUND TWO MEETINGS

Congratulations!

The finish line is clearly in front of you. You have considered all your options for getting the best win-win outcome from this important negotiation. You have the person who is authorized to do a deal with you. Now let's start the next round in the negotiation for rebate process. Let's do this deal.

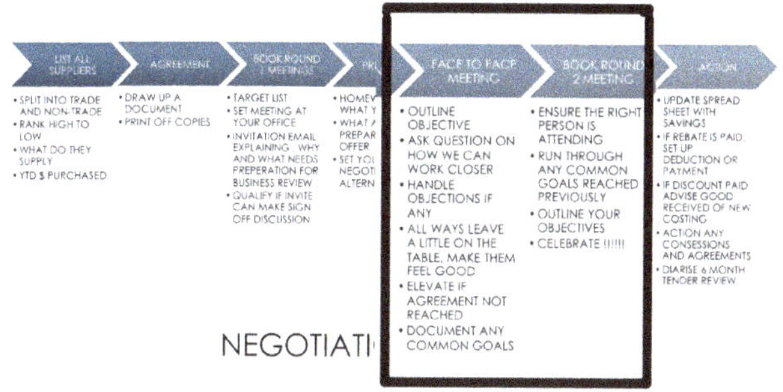

Many business owners want to be important to their suppliers - the big fish in a small pond. They want to have a relationship that is not just a transaction. Owners also want their business seen as being important to their suppliers' futures.

This reminds me of a story that will demonstrate this point.

As national marketing and promotions manager for one of Australia's largest food and beverage wholesale companies, I had organized a large corporate event in Las Vegas, Nevada. With me were the 25 leading suppliers to Australia's largest fast moving consumer goods wholesaler. We had just finished a lavish dinner in the Palms Casino. Little did they know what I had planned for the evening ahead! Our next stop was Hugh Heffner's 75th birthday party! To make the evening even more memorable, we were given a table next to Hugh and all of his Playboy Bunnies!

Everyone had their cell phones out, taking selfies and calling their friends back in Australia with comments like "you are never going to believe where I am to-night" and "I can't believe who I just meet".

The Australian Consumer goods market was and still is to this day, dominated by big corporate public companies. The company that I was working for supplied the Independent Retail Supermarkets, which was number three in terms of market shares at that time.

We were the small fish in a very large pond. I knew that the suppliers who were present at Hugh Heffner's 75th birthday party represented 80% of goods sold. These people had massive influence over our destinies.

As you can imagine, the negotiations that followed were not overly difficult.

Through events like these, we negotiated hard but fair. We changed our mindset about being a small fish in a big pond. Instead, we became a company that wanted to align our future plans with our suppliers, and it worked.

The relationships we developed gave us a positive improvement to our rebate income 100% of the time. Without the process I am sharing with you, I do not believe that there would have been the level of trust and mutual respect that exists.

The take-a-way I wish to leave you with is this: Negotiations with win-win outcomes build relationships that last. Your future will depend on a few factors, and one is how well you build relationships with your key suppliers.

One of the concerns that my case study client Alice had, as she prepared for her round two negotiations, was that her suppliers would increase their prices to offset whatever her gains from them were. Therefore, it is worth spending a few paragraphs on putting these concerns aside.

First, it is true that it could happen. However, let me point out a few ways around this issue to make sure that it does not.

Number one, every year you must have an annual review for your business or this category within your business. This doesn't mean you are going to change your suppliers; however, they need to understand that this time next year you are going to ask another company to come in and make you an offer to become your supplier.

What you are not going to disclose to the potential new supplier is the rebate that you are getting from your present supplier. That, my friend, has to be the best kept secret in your company.

Number two, a rebate is not shown on an invoice. This is very important for your supplier.
They don't want your competitor, or anybody else, to know the deal that they are about to do with you.

The reason why we ask for a rebate in the first place is that we do not want any discount to be shown on an invoice. I can't tell you how many times I have found out that a supplier was paying a higher rebate to my competitors. The only way to get this information without having to buy out your competition, is if the discount is written on an invoice and it falls into the wrong person's hands.

Number three, if there is a corporate business in your town, I most likely can guarantee you that they are getting paid a discount in the form of a rebate.

If you have a Woolworths owned hospitality business (the market leader for consumer goods in Australia) as your competition for example, it is written on their supplier agreements, which anyone can download off their website, the "ask for discount" and a guarantee they will always buy at the suppliers' lowest prices. Woolworths doesn't hide the fact that rebate payments are part of the conditions of doing business with them and will leverage their buying power if it is ever discovered that their prices are not competitive.

Once your negotiations have been finalised, you will have real buying power. Remember, we are working towards having you be a big fish in a little pond.

This is what happened for Alice from A1 Hospitality.

Alice systematically worked her way through her list of vendors and committed 3 weeks where she would have face to face negotiations.

I impressed on Alice the importance of holding those meetings on her premises and not her suppliers' places of business. That way she could feel more confident in the environment and could take the vendor on a tour of what she was building, before sitting down to negotiate.

Alice made sure that the vendor was aware of why they were meeting and that they had the authority to negotiate with her without the need of someone else to sign the agreement.

She opened with a summarization of the previous round one meeting and then got down to the business of asking for a 10% discount paid as a rebate.

Not all of Alice's meetings ended in a **YES.** Also, she did have to ask her vendors what they needed for them to say **YES**. There was some give and take necessary, however, as the meetings were finalized, she began to calculate her savings and saw that they were significant.

I remember Alice saying, "Chris, this is really working". The dollar value Alice had negotiated for was a staggering $130,000 annualised rebates on her $970,000 purchases. This was a 13.40% saving on her cost of goods, not just for one year, but for every year!

As mentioned, some of Alice's meetings did end in a **NO**. Since not every negotiation will get a **YES**, we need to know what to do next if the meeting goes pear-shaped.

Respect is only earned, and every action has to have a reaction. Alice had to cut suppliers, she had to change some favourable trading relationships to un-favourable, and some needed to be escalated up to a higher authority. The take-a-way is that once you start, you can't stop. That is the key to a negotiation.

It is the same idea when buying a new car. Either both parties can agree to the terms or not. As a customer, sometimes you must just walk away and go someplace else. You don't decide not to buy a car if you get a **NO**. In that case, the car salesperson knows that you won't be back and has to be comfortable with that. Perhaps that is why the best car deals are done at the end of the month when the salesperson's numbers need a boost to get their bonus.

A negotiation is not completed until the agreement is documented and signed by both parties. This is your trading term agreement.

A point to note: This is an agreement that you are drawing up, not a contract. The difference is a contract cannot be changed without having legal review, which is costly and unnecessary. Either party can make alterations to an agreement as long as each part agrees and initials the changes.

Having a formal documentation process positions your business as professional and you will need this level of professionalism as you grow.

CHAPTER NINE

YOU ARE ONLY AS GOOD AS YOUR LAST DEAL

"Just because you make a good plan, doesn't mean that's what's gonna happen." Taylor Swift

NEGOTIATION PROCESS

If everyone in your organization doesn't execute the conditions in the trading term agreement, everything that you've been negotiating for can be wasted. There is no excuse for poor communication. In good faith, your vendor agreed to pay your business a rebate and, in most negotiations, you offered something of low value to you and high value to the vendor. Your reputation is now squarely on the line. Will you deliver on what you agreed to do? Your weakest link is your ability to communicate with your team what is now expected.

Build communication into your training. Have a process for explaining your new agreements. For example, you don't share with your employees what you are getting, just that you have made a deal with the supplier and from this week, they are the only supplier you will be buying from.

This reminds me of the story about a husband and wife who hired a marketing agency to increase sales for their company. They invested a total of $8000 into a marketing campaign and got no return and no difference whatsoever in their revenue. The couple then tried to figure out why this happened. The wife said "I don't understand. You gave the marketing agency all the details on our target market, what could possibly have gone wrong?". The husband then said, "I didn't give the agency the target market details, I thought you did!" Assuming that the other had followed through, cost this husband-and-wife team a lot of money. Make sure this doesn't happen with you!

Let's for a minute go back to my client, Alice. One of her biggest concerns when this process started was hurting her reputation.

The lack of follow through and execution of what you have negotiated is what damages your reputation. It is not that you were too tough in what you asked for, it's that you did not honour the deal you shook hands on. I think you can see the importance of this.

The communication to your accounts department must be flawless, for example.

A deal that you just made can be undone the first time that your payment is late. This is what your vendor is going to remember – they have done a deal with you in good faith, and it hasn't happened.

My experience as a buyer for wholesalers and retailers was to never over commit.

Never say **YES** to a deal that you know you can't honour, as it will hurt your reputation.

Here is an opportunity to cement your relationship with your vendors and to create raving fans. Your vendors have friends and family as well. They could be your customers right now. They could be dining in your restaurant, they could be drinking in your pub. There will be a lot of word-of-mouth goodwill created when they say "I did a deal with Alice at A1 Hospitality Hotel and they have honoured their agreement flawlessly. This business really has their act together. We need to deal with more people like Alice."

I have made errors and said **YES** in negotiations when I should have said **NO**. You don't have to repeat these errors.

There is a wise saying that smart people learn from their mistakes and that smarter people learn from the mistakes of others!

It is now time to document how you will communicate the agreements you have reached to the key members of your team.

Your trading term agreements need to be filed in a secure place away from access to all but your key team members. Do not share the discounts with anyone who doesn't need to know.

Make sure you have confirmed the agreement with your vendor via email and that both parties have a copy.

CHAPTER TEN

LEVERAGE YOUR BUYING POWER

Let me first be the first to congratulate you. Well done!

You have stayed true to the process. You have learned new skills and your team has executed your trading terms agreements flawlessly. You have also scheduled your annual review next year.

However, like trees, if your business is not growing, it's dying. So how can we leverage your buying power? Where's the low hanging fruit in your business operation? You can invest your rebate money, or a part of this new income stream, into more revenue creating strategies.

There is nothing wrong with taking your rebate money to the bank. Let's face it though, the more you earn, the more you spend. We will always buy on emotions and justify it with logic.

Purchase a new vehicle if that is what your business needs, however, consider some other possibilities.

Money has an energy all of its own and you may have heard the expression "money makes money".

Think about your rebate money as bank interest. What can you invest all, or part, of your rebate payments into, that will generate new revenue opportunities? The more revenue you can generate, the more goods your business will need to purchase. Think of a jet plane taking off. It takes energy to get off the ground, however once the plane is in the air, it doesn't require massive energy to get it to fly higher. It is the same in your business.

The more revenue you can create, the more interest you earn, and it keeps compounding as it accumulates.

Think about some of the really inspirational people in business. Sir Richard Branson is on the top of my list.

I often asked myself "What would Richard Branson do in this situation? Would he take the newfound income to the bottom-line profit or would he re-invest it into other revenue generating investments?"

Who in the business world inspires you? In your situation, what would they do with this newfound buying power?

Say, for example, you own a restaurant and have decided to invest in a wood-fired pizza oven. Realistically, you are using the vendor's money (paid to you as a rebate) to create more revenue for yourself. That is true buying power!

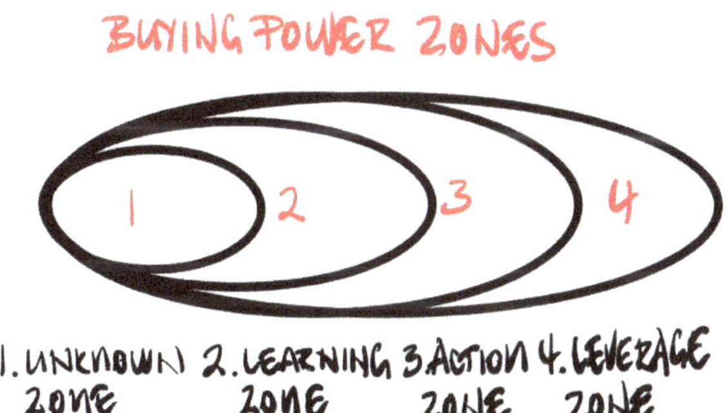

What are some other things you might look at? Does your hospitality company have any event business? If so, what events do you get; how can you attract more of these or increase their frequency and/or quality; what events are going to your competition?

Always remember, MONEY MAKES MONEY – it is the Law of Attraction. You have a new income stream in the form of your rebate payments from your vendors. This money will attract more money, if you allow it to do its work.

Now let's look at how Alice from A1 Hospitality generated $980,000 in new business by reinvesting her rebate money into new ventures.

Alice was aware that, although there was no shortage of wedding venues and even a conference centre nearby, there were no really great five-star event locations in her marketplace.

Her fine dining restaurant was in a perfect location and could hold large corporate events up to 1000 people. Her venue could also work well for events such as a new car launch, for example.

The usual menu choices for conference gala dinners are often a standard choice of beef or chicken. Although this can work for a lot of budgets, it generally isn't very interesting.

Alice and her team knew they had something unique to offer, that no one else was tapping into. Now she had to figure out how she was going to attract the clients. I suggested that Alice make a list of all the event managers and management companies in her town. Which of these managers did she know personally, and which ones didn't she know?

This is where we started to have a lot of fun.

I challenged Alice to take her head chef with her to meet with these event managers.

To make each of these meetings memorable, I suggested they take along a gift that would demonstrate some of their creative skills. With this in mind, the chef baked some beautiful cupcakes and he and Alice took a box to each of the event managers. At these meetings, Alice described her unique venue and invited them to a site inspection the following week.

Remember, the objective of a first meeting is to get to the second meeting.

At no point were they trying to sell anything.

Having the chef attend with Alice indicated to the managers that he had a vested interest in the success of the business.

Now, to really make a statement to her potential event manager partners, Alice invited everyone for a site inspection at the same time. This way she was really able to show case what she had to offer. Since event management is a very competitive industry, Alice was creating a sense of urgency in the managers' minds where they all wanted to be the first to book her venue for their VIP clients.

Exactly as we learned, this was Alice's round one. Round two is where you meet with them again. This is where I coached Alice to really get smart with her negotiations.

I suggested she offer a rebate to the event management business to bring business to her. Remember, they make their money by "clipping the ticket" and by adding a margin for their service to the raw cost. Alice wanted their business, so she told them she was prepared to pay a rebate on the total invoice value they spent with her. Since she was already collecting rebates of between 10% and 13%, she offered them 5%.

This is how A1 Hospitality was able to generate $980,000 in new business.

More purchases drive more rebate dollars, thus increasing the size of the pie, which in turn makes for happier vendors, and a happier community as your business grows. This is where buying power is so important for your future.

CHAPTER 11

THE VALUE OF A BUSINESS PLAN

If it's in your head, it's dead. In other words, you need to get your thoughts and ideas out of your head and get them onto one document.

What is success for you? How do you know when you are there?

A business plan is a tool that will give you feedback as to whether you are on track to achieving the success you are planning for. Think of it as a Google Maps navigation system. If you stray off your route, take a wrong turn, or take a route to your destination that is blocked by heavy traffic, Google Maps will help you get back on course.

All big corporate businesses got to where they are today because they had a plan and a strategy that they followed.

Let's look at the reason you went into your hospitality business. The reasons that most people go into business are to make a good living, to be their own boss and eventually sell or pass it on to their family.

Would you like to say to a potential buyer "Here is my business plan, and this is where we are up to on the plan. Now all you need to do is follow the bouncing ball to achieve these business goals". How powerful and confident would you feel being able to make this statement?

The reason I hear most for not having a documented business plan, is that it is a lot of work to create one. However, I would like to share with you why I think that they are well worth the time and effort.

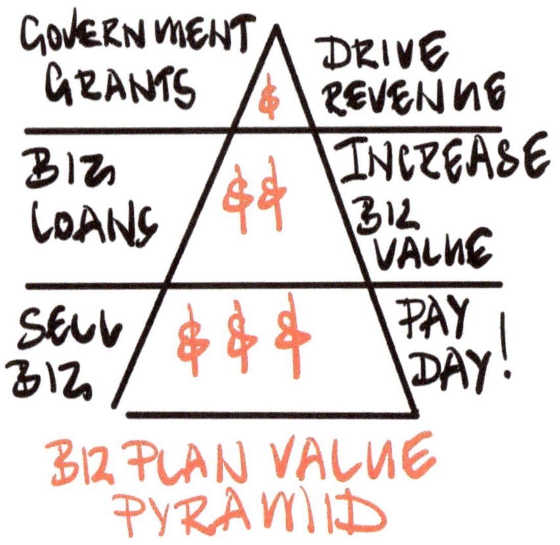

Number One - Government Grants.

At this point on our journey, you now have buying power and you are leveraging it in many ways to create new business opportunities. One opportunity that you may not have considered is government grants.

Let me tell you, there are government grants for nearly everything. A business plan is certainly going to help you win your application for one of these grants. My client Alice used a documented plan to apply for and get $150,000 as part of a tourism development grant. With this money, she developed a unique offer that drove more revenue and more purchases, which in turn kept growing the rebate payments from her suppliers.

Number Two - Bank Loans.

As your business expands you are going to need more financing and, inevitably, you are going to need to go to the bank. A detailed business plan will give you the best chance to secure the funding.

Number Three - Investors / New Partners.

At this point, perhaps you are considering bringing in an investor or new partner, or even selling your company. As previously mentioned, having a detailed business plan will show them where your company currently stands and where it is heading, and give them the confidence in you and your ability to deliver.

In chapter five of my book "Cashing Out With Confidence", I explain business plans in much greater detail. I encourage you to read this book for a better understanding of how and why they work so well.

Michael Gerber, author of the book "The E Myth", underscores the need to work **ON** your business, not **IN** it. The time and energy that you invest into a business plan is working **ON** your business.

In my coaching business, I have guided scores of clients through the process of creating a business plan. Studies have shown, and it has been my own experience, that companies with documented plans have much better success than companies without them.

Psychology professor, Dr. Gail Matthews, recruited 267 people from varying backgrounds to participate in a study on how goal achievement in the workplace is influenced by three key actions: Writing goals, committing to goal-directed actions, and lastly, creating accountability for those actions.

Dr. Matthews created five groups for this study. Group one was told to simply think about their goals. Group two through five took progressively greater initiatives to support their efforts. Results grew from 43 percent success rate in group one and escalated to 76 percent in group five, as reported by Inc.com in their article on January 28, 2019.

A business plan is used to help manage an organisation by stating ambitions, how they will be achieved, and exactly when. Your business plan will serve as a key point of reference for investors, partners, employees, and management to gauge progress against objectives.

In closing, this book has given you a lot to take in and a lot more to action.

You have learned how to negotiate with your vendors and suppliers for rebate payments, which have reduced your cost of goods.

You understand that if you follow the process, it works. As a result of your new-found negotiating skills, your relationships with your suppliers have been strengthened.

With some or all of your rebate payments, you have invested in new revenue-generating opportunities. You have also learned to leverage your buying power to attract event business that you were not previously considered for.

Lastly, we have tied all of the steps in this book together with a documented business plan that you can use to sell your business; bring partners or investors in; apply for bank financing; and receive government stimulus grants.

Even though you may not be on the same playing field as the large corporate giants in the hospitality industry when it comes to the number of outlets you have, your business can remain competitive. The pressure of your cost of goods being constantly pushed up can be offset when you increase and then leverage your buying power and find new ways for your business to thrive.

EXCITING INFO

We have a coaching program developed to guide business owners in the hospitality industry in implementing the process detailed in this book.

Would you like to join us?

P.S. Whenever you're ready, here are 4 ways I can help you grow your business:

1. Connect with me on Facebook at

https://www.facebook.com/Mackeybizcoach

2. Subscribe to my YouTube channel for up-to-date guidance and tactics on the five ways to grow any business:

https://www.youtube.com/results?search_query=chrisBIZCOACH

3. Follow me on LinkedIn:

https://www.linkedin.com/in/action-coachchrismackey/

4. Visit my website:

https://chrismackey.actioncoach.com/

P.P.S. If you're ready now, book a time for a conversation

https://calendly.com/chrismackey60/22-min-discovery-session

www.ingramcontent.com/pod-product-compliance
Lightning Source LLC
Chambersburg PA
CBHW050011040726
47599CB00014B/1330